Haines for All Seasons

Northern Exposures from Alaska--
Reflecting Our Bond with the Land and Each Other

by Kathleen M.K. Menke

Dedicated to all my relations,
in this valley and beyond,
in memory of my father, James E. Kennell,
who also loved Alaska

All Photos/Contents ©Kathleen M.K. Menke/Crystal Images

Published and Distributed by Crystal Images
PO Box 781, Haines, Alaska 99827   907-766-3517
Website: www.akmk.com   E-mail: ci@akmk.com

ISBN 0-9764261-0-2
First Edition 2005
Printed in China through InterPress Limited

To order additional books or individual photos, contact Crystal Images--contact information listed above.
For more information about Haines, Alaska, the Haines Visitor Center website is: www.haines.ak.us

Thank you to all who have provided input, encouragement,
technical support, and permissions for this project.

This book is designed with minimal text to allow readers their own memories, stories,
interpretations, and/or dreams. Photo captions each page read left to right, top to bottom.
KmKm

Cover Photos: Bald Eagle Calling/Chilkat Bald Eagle Preserve; Haines, Alaska/Chilkat Range from Nukdik Point;
Alaska Coastal Brown Bear Siblings/Lutak; Spawning Sockeye Salmon/Bear Creek/Upper Chilkoot Watershed

Haines, Alaska, is...

Haines, Alaska/Ft. William H. Seward National Historic Landmark/Chilkat Range Reflection from Nukdik Point

...the beginning of the trail and the end of the trail--"Dei-shu"

Hiker Jake Menke/Haines Peninsula from Mt. Ripinsky; Lynn Canal from Mt. Riley; Seven-Mile Saddle/East Chilkoot Range; Shoreline/Trail from Battery Point; Rainbow Glacier/Chilkat Range/Moose Meadows/Seduction Point Trail

Rainwater on Ice/Chilkoot Lake/February; Looking South from Canoe/Chilkoot Lake; Fisherpeople/Chilkoot River;
Lone Fisherperson/Chilkoot Lake; Winter Scene/Chilkoot River

...and Chilkat reflections

Rainbow Glacier/Chilkat Range/Chilkat Inlet Reflection; Chilkat River Looking South to Coastal Mountains;
Autumn Reflection/Chilkat/Haines Highway; Still Morning Reflection/Chilkat Inlet; Mt. Ripinsky/Chilkat River/ Winter

...where bears catch wild salmon, play, and roam peacefully among us

Brown Bear with Pink Salmon/Lutak; Young Brown Bears Wrestling in Tall Grass/Chilkoot; Brown Bear Siblings/Lutak

Sow and Three Yearlings/Chilkoot; Good Scratch/Chilkoot; Grizzly in Dandelions/Near Klukwan; Along Back Road/Klukwan

...with more than a hint of Northern Exposure

Autumn Moose/Center of Town; Relaxing/Small Boat Harbor Pavilion;
Walking the Walk/Mountain Market; In Alder Patch/Along Front Street

Trumpeter Swans in Flight; Raft of Scoters/Lynn Canal; Northern White-Fronted Geese/Chilkat Pond;
Great Blue Heron and Reflection/Waterfront; Pair of Barrow's Goldeneyes; Snow Geese/Portage Cove

Scenes from Chilkat Bald Eagle Preserve: Bald Eagle Calling; Juvenile Bald Eagle; Competition

Council Grounds Tree; In Flight Over Chilkoot; Juvenile Sunning Its Wings; Gathering/Chilkat Flats

...nestled in a spruce and hemlock forest

3920 Peak/Haines Peninsula from 7-Mile Saddle Trail;
Backlit Spruce/Winter; Port Chilkoot Subdivision/Mud Bay Road/Chilkat River/Chilkat Range

Mountain Hemlock/Mt. Riley; Devil's Club; Usnea/Old Man's Beard; Driftwood/Forest/Battery Point Trail;
Spring Spruce Tips; Autumn Forest Ground Cover/Mosquito Lake; Tommy Jimmie/Sitka Spruce/Upper Chilkoot

Coastal Mountains from Chilkoot; Haines/Chilkat Range/From Lynn Canal

Coastal Mountains from Mud Bay Road; Cathedral Peaks; Davidson Glacier/Waterfront/Chilkat Mountains;
Haines Surrounded; Rainbow Glacier; Davidson Glacier Face; Letnikof Cove/Coastal Mountains

Waterfront View/Coastal Mountains; Storm Surf/Tanani Bay

Sea Lion Rock/Lynn Canal; Haines Coastline/Chilkat Range; Shoreline/Portage Cove;
Lutak Inlet Reflection/Chilkoot Range; Waterfront Reflection/Coastal Mountains; Mud Bay View; Winter Ice/Lutak Inlet

17

...beneath dancing lights

Rare Red Aurora; Northern Lights Over Little House on Peninsula; City Lights/Northern Lights

The Lights Danced and the Wolves Sang/Midnight/Confluence Tatshenshini and Klukshu Rivers

...where people can still gather their own food from the land and sea

Coleus Taylor Gathering Dulse; Nancy McCallum Gathering Oyster Leaf; Goose Tongue Growing on Chilkat Beach; Debi Knight Kennedy Gathering Crow Berries and Blueberries on Chilkat Pass; Bucket of Alpine Crow Berries

Sunset/Cathedral Peaks/Subsistence Salmon Gill Net/Chilkat River; Cara Lawrence and Renee Hebert Crabbing/Mud Bay; Jake Menke with Dinner/Pink Salmon/Chilkoot River; Norm Hughes/Bringing Home Deer

...home to the hooligan (eulachon) harvest

Spring Hooligan Havest/Chilkoot (All): Brown Bear; Sea Lions; Ernie Wilkins Dipnetting; Flora Beierly Teaching Granddaughter Janine Phillips; Eagle Searching; Close-up Hooligan; Frying on the Beach; Gulls Gathered; Eagle Waiting

Paul Wilson; Wilson's Smokehouse; At 4-Mile along Chilkat River: Shoveling Fermented Hooligan from Pit; Stirring the Simmering Vat; Marilyn Wilson and Steve Hay/Skimming Oil; Elsie Mellott and Abby Strong/Chilkoot; Sarah Posey/Carr's Cove

...a community of individuals with unique talents and skills, generously shared

Norm Hughes/Net Hanging Blues; Buster Benson at His Sawmill; Dan Humphrey with Fresh Birch Syrup from the Still;
Suzi McCollum/Children/Puppets/Sheldon Museum; Ray Menaker/Spinner of Yarns; Rachel "Dixie" Johnson/Tlingit Art;
Ed Beitner/Gatherer of Pixies/Chilkoot; Joe Ordonez and Mike Speaks/River Guides; Dave Pahl/Hammer Collection

Logging Contest/Southeast Alaska State Fair; John Svenson Painting Mural at American Bald Eagle Foundation;
Tlingit Park Playground Volunteers(2): Father Jim Blaney/Norm Blank Check Supplies; Teen Girls Digging Post Hole;
Beth McCready and Customers/Popcorn Stand; John Hagen and Wayne Price Carving Totem/Alaska Indian Arts

...a place for children and families

Tlingit Park Community-Built Playground: Isaiah May; Donna and Grace Lambert; Towers and Tunnel; Skye and Sarah Posey:
Boys Fishing Chilkoot River; SE AK State Fair: Cynthia, Elizabeth, and Janine Phillips; Jo Feldman Holding Tiaya Ruggierello

Joseph Marks/4th of July; Jack Griffith/Skunk Cabbage Patch; Dawson Evenden and Jasper Posey with Float;
Schwartz/Whitermore Family Outing/Battery Point; March Outing/Boys/Tanani Point

...where cultural traditions endure

Repatriated Murrelet Hat/Kaagwaantaan Clan; Harry Johnson Holding His Son, Dante; Paulina Phillips and Lillian Hammond

John Hagen Carving Totem/Alaska Indian Arts; Charlie and Verna Jimmie/Eagle Release/Chilkat Bald Eagle Preserve;
Keely Falcon and Deborah Asper/Chilkat Dancers; Klukwan Chilkats/Alaska Native Sisterhood Hall/Klukwan

Norwegian Cruises/Nighttime Visit/Portage Cove; Visitors Disembarking AMH State Ferries/Haines Terminal (2);
Visitors/Chilkat Bald Eagle Preserve; Bart Henderson Assists Visitors/Glacier Point; Steve Kroschel/Coyote/His Wildllife Park

Hotel Halsingland; Salmon Bake; Yellow Transparent Apple Tree in Bloom/Sheldon Museum and Cultural Center;
Nels Niemi/Senior River Guide/Tatshenshini River; Main Street/Winter; Mountain Market//Winter

Haines Small Boat Harbor and Crow; Bruce Gilbert's Ferry, M/V Silver Eagle, and Fishing Boats /Letnikof Harbor Reflection

Small Boat Harbor; Monte/Kayak/Battery Point; Art Jess/Bayliner; Bill Thomas/F/V Raven's Walk; Jeannie Henry/King Crab; Bill Jackson and Paul Wilson/Hanging Salmon Gill Net/Carr's Cove; Letnikof Harbor/Winter; Good Partner II/Portage Cove

M/V Columbia Lynn Canal; Eldred Rock Lighthouse; M/V Malaspina/Fireweed/Lutak; Comraderie on Deck/Rainbow;
Folk Festival Musicians; Ferry Wake; Glacier View from Ferry; Relaxing on Sundeck; Peaceful Morning; Fairbanks Musicians

...part of the network of Southeast Alaska communities

Approaching Wrangell; Russian Orthodox Church/Sitka; Ketchikan Totems; Creek Street/Ketchikan; Whale Petroglyph/Wrangell; Sitka Blacktail Deer; Capitol Building/Juneau; Mendenhall Glacier/Juneau; Calving Glacier/Tracy Arm; Tenakee Springs

Lenise Henderson Overlooking Confluence Tatshenshini and Alsek Rivers; Willow Ptarmigan Pair/Chilkat Pass; Coyote/Yukon; Sunset Tanana River/Tetlin Preserve; Autumn/Kluane Lake; Kluane World Heritage Site (2): Slims River; Kaskawulsh Glacier

Samuel Glacier/Chilkat Pass; Clearwater Creek/Denali Highway; Denali Mother; Denali Range/Reflection Pond

...an integral part of the "Golden Circle"

Off Haines Highway: BC Mountains near US/Canada Border; X-C Skiing/Chilkat Pass; Autumn/Three Guardsmen Peaks;
Yukon: Gaffing Sockeye/Klukshu Village; Historical Cabin/Champagne; Miles Canyon/Yukon River/Near Whitehorse

Carcross Ice Cream Parlor; Emerald Lake/Yukon; Klondike Steamer/Yukon River/Whitehorse; Tagish Lake/Yukon; Chilkoot Trail Hikers/Arctic Brotherhood Hall/Skagway; Fireweed/White Pass

...where the water is clean and the air is pure

M/V Columbia/Lynn Canal; Chuck Creek/Samuel Glacier; Sockeye Spawning Area/West Side Chilkoot Lake

Sunset/Portage Cove; Sunset/Cathedral Peaks/Chilkat River;
Ted Buel/Haines Highway Spring; Mark Higgins/Mud Bay Road Spring

...where salmon, still wild, return

Spawning Sockeye/Bear Creek/Upper Chilkoot Watershed; Glory Hole with Spawning Sockeye/Upper Chilkoot Watershed; Pink Salmon/Chilkoot River; Late Season Chum Salmon/Chilkat River

...nourishing the multitudes

Bald Eagles Dining/Chilkat River Council Grounds/Klukwan; Brown Bear Family Salmon Fishing/Chilkoot River

New Growth/Island Rock/Chilkoot River; Bald Eagle Feeding on Sea Lion Carcass/Front Street Beach

...and to dust returns

Salmon Bones/Chilkoot; Moose Antler/Tatshenshini; Bald Eagle Feather/North Chilkoot Beach; Chum Salmon Skull/Chilkat

...a place of abundance for all seasons

Fireweed (3); Skunk Cabbage; Shooting Stars; M. Plucker/Garden; Chilkoot Lake/Winter; Paintbrush/Forget-Me-Nots/Lupine; Brown Bear Family Hooligan Fishing; Thanksgiving Day/Chilkat River; Bald Eagle/Snowy Branches; Hoarfrost/Chilkoot

Crow with Mountain Ash Berry; Autumn Tundra: Red Bear-Berry and Green Crow-Berry Foliage; Local Pie Cherries; Autumn Tundra: Reindeer Moss and Lingonberry; Winter Scene/Porcupine Bridge/Chilkat Range

...unfolding anew each day

Spring Ice Fringe/Chilkat River